Winning Souls Step-By-Step

Your step-by-step guide to win souls, bring guests to church, and baptize converts.

Paul E Chapman

Winning Souls Step-By-Step

Your step-by-step guide to win souls, bring guests to church, and baptize converts.

By Paul E Chapman

Published by:
Add To Your Faith Publications
P.O. Box 5369
S. Kingstown, RI, USA

Bulk Discounts Available At AddToYourFaith.com.

Printed in USA

Winning Souls Step-By-Step

Well Done!

You are reading this book because you have a burden to see people saved. This book is an excerpt from a larger work entitled "Winning Souls God's Way: A Manual For Confident Soul Winning."

If you would like to further your soul-winning training to increase your effectiveness winning the lost, you can purchase our entire soul-winning manual at AddToYourFaith.com. It will be available in the Fall of 2024. Also, you can sign up for soul winning tips at soulwinningschool.com.

May Almighty God empower you to see many souls saved for His eternal glory!

Let's Connect...

You can connect with the author by subscribing to updates at **PaulEChapman.com** and following him on social media platforms by the handle **@thepaulechapman**.

Winning Souls Step-By-Step

Introduction

Matthew 28:18–20

"And Jesus came and spake unto them, saying, All power is given unto me in heaven and in earth. Go ye therefore, and teach all nations, baptizing them in the name of the Father, and of the Son, and of the Holy Ghost: Teaching them to observe all things whatsoever I have commanded you: and, lo, I am with you alway, even unto the end of the world. Amen."

The Great Commission was Christ's last command on Earth. He established it to be the ongoing mission of His followers. On the evening of the Resurrection, Christ met with His disciples to give them marching orders. He would be leaving soon to go back to Heaven, but His mission to save the lost must continue. He commanded His devotees to go into all the world preaching His soul-saving message. Unfortunately today, many believers treat Christ's Great Commission more like the Great Suggestion.

When I was a young man, I heard the preacher talk about the Great Commission many times. Each time I heard about it, I sat in church and gave God all the reasons why it didn't apply to me.

- I was an introvert.
- I didn't know enough Bible.
- That was the preacher's job.
- I didn't want to bother people.
- People would think I was nuts.

Pastor Ross preached often about our responsibility to reach the lost. He would say things like, "How many times does God need to say something in order for it to be important? Once. How often must God command us before we obey? One time."

God repeats Himself in the Bible for emphasis. At times, He confirms His commandments with repetition. This fact doesn't make the items He mentions once of less importance, but it elevates the commands He repeats.

The Great Commission is so important that it is reiterated in all four Gospels and the Book of Acts. Examine each instance.

Mark 16:15

"And he said unto them, Go ye into all the world, and preach the gospel to every creature."

Luke 24:47–48

"And that repentance and remission of sins should be

preached in his name among all nations, beginning at Jerusalem. And ye are witnesses of these things."

John 20:21

"Then said Jesus to them again, Peace be unto you: as my Father hath sent me, even so send I you."

Acts 1:8

"But ye shall receive power, after that the Holy Ghost is come upon you: and ye shall be witnesses unto me both in Jerusalem, and in all Judaea, and in Samaria, and unto the uttermost part of the earth."

As a sixteen-year-old, those convicting words finally got through my thick skull. Most of the planet was going to Hell and God commanded me to do something about it. Eventually, God broke down all my excuses. I surrendered to my responsibility to reach the lost. I wanted to be a soul winner.

Now I had a new problem. I didn't know how to win souls! I didn't even know where to begin!

Thankfully, I was brought to Christ through the bus ministry of Blessed Hope Baptist Church in Jasonville, Indiana. This miracle church is a soul-winning and evangelistic lighthouse that cares for sinners and preaches the Gospel fearlessly among dozens of small towns surrounded by corn fields and cow pastures.

Pastor Robert Ross and Pastor Jerry Ross taught me how to win souls. Bro. Bo Eikelman was my bus captain and Sunday School teacher. I watched him sacrifice his time every Saturday striving to reach boys, girls, and families for

Winning Souls Step-By-Step

Jesus. I am grateful that I had tremendous examples of how to bring people to Jesus.

Pastor Jerry Ross not only took me soul winning personally, but he exposed me to the books, sermons, and ministries of some of the greatest soul winners in history. By God's grace, I was winning souls to Christ each week before I went to Bible College. I was walking converts down the aisle regularly. I had become a soul winner! If God can make a young country boy from the rural Midwest a soul winner, He can do the same for you!

I have been winning souls for thirty years. There is no greater joy than winning a soul to Christ. The soul winner gets the privilege of watching the miracle of the new birth take place. We are the spiritual nurses assisting the Great Physician birth His redeemed children. We get to see the Holy Spirit change hearts. We witness the first glimmers of eternal life as their eyes light up with joy. Becoming a consistent soul winner will be the most exciting journey of your life.

This booklet is written to help you become a proficient and consistent soul winner. With God's help, you can make an eternal difference by rescuing lost souls from Hell's eternal flame. God does all the saving. He is the Miracle Worker. He simply needs a voice to share His life-changing message of love, sacrifice, and salvation.

You are reading this book because you want to become a soul winner. Congratulations! A desire to learn and grow is the first step to this worthy goal.

Also in this book, you will learn how to give your converts Biblical assurance of salvation, get them to church, walk them down the aisle to profess Christ, see them baptized, and start them on the road to discipleship.

God created the Universe to run according to laws. Creation exists in harmony because it obeys God's natural laws. We experience the blessings of a good family by obeying God's laws of relationships. Business success comes when we identify and obey God's laws of work. Evangelism is no different.

You will become a successful personal soul winner when you learn and obey the Bible's principles regarding soul winning. These principles are not new. They have been taught and proven for generations. This step-by-step guide encapsulates God's laws of evangelism and the best practices of effective soul winners into an easy-to-follow process. You will win sinners to Jesus consistently by observing this practical advice.

This guide is broken up into three groups of 44 sections. Sections 1-21 prepare you to go soul winning with the correct approach. Sections 22-33 teach you exactly what to say to win a soul to Christ. Sections 34-44 explain how to work with your new converts, encouraging them to follow Christ.

Telling someone about Jesus is not difficult. Don't allow the number of sections to discourage you. Many of them of short. We use sections to make this material easy to teach, study, and retain.

Each section begins on a right-hand page for ease of use. Blank pages are intended to be used for your notes.

Let's get started!

1

Set A Definite Time To Go

Scheduling a time to go soul winning is a simple yet vital step to becoming a consistent soul winner. No one becomes a soul winner by accident. You must decide to win souls and commit to doing whatever is necessary to keep that commitment.

Of course, we should be constant witnesses throughout our day as we go about our business. That is the difference between going soul winning and being a soul winner. However, something unique happens when you put an item on your schedule. That simple action moves the item from a "hope" to a commitment in your heart. Things that get scheduled get done. If you don't have a scheduled time to win people to Christ, you probably won't.

It is wise to go during the soul-winning time scheduled at your church. You will not only commit to a specific time each week, but also, you will encourage the heart of your pastor. If your church does not have an organized soul-winning program, plan your own time to go.

Allow me to give you a word of encouragement. My flesh never wants to go soul winning. What? The guy writing a soul-winning book doesn't want to go soul winning?? Let's get real. We are made of the same clay. Every Christian has similar battles. If you wait for a feeling, you will rarely leave the comfort of your home in search of sinners.

Many of the great soul winners in history testify that they fought desperately to overcome insecurity, shyness, unbelief, and apathy. Most Christians don't "feel" like going soul winning. Soul winning is spiritual, and the flesh will fight against it. Satan will do everything he can to keep you from spreading the good news of the Gospel. Soul winning is not a feeling for which we wait. It is a command to be obeyed.

I rarely want to go soul winning at first, but I don't want to stop once I get going! The key is to go. Set a time. Open your mouth. Talk to the first person you see. Allow the Holy Spirit to start working through you, and you won't want to stop.

Every Christian should have a set time during the week to go soul winning.

2

Be Soul Conscious

Decent Christians fail to witness for one simple reason. They are not conscious of souls. I truly believe that the average Christian would witness regularly if they were aware of the spiritual ramifications of the moment.

What does it mean to be soul conscious? It means that we never lose sight of the fact that everyone has a soul. The vast multitudes are lost. That fact means that most of the people you meet in your life are one heartbeat away from eternal damnation. What a terrible thought! We must not shy away from the burden of reaching them before it is too late.

A soul conscious Christian strives to witness to as many people as he can. He carries tracts intending to pass them out. He looks for ways to bring up the Lord or turn the conversation toward the Saviour. The store clerk, the barber, the mechanic, the coworker, and the gas station attendant need the Lord. You cannot witness to the wrong person because everyone has a soul, and Christ died for everyone.

Great soul winners have always been attuned to the needs of sinners around them. Consider the following story about D.L. Moody.

> *"When Dwight L. Moody was in London during one of his famous evangelistic tours, several British clergymen visited him. They wanted to know how and why this poorly educated American was so effective in winning throngs of people to Christ. Moody took the three men to the window of his hotel room and asked each in turn what he saw. One by one, the men described the people in the park below. Then Moody looked out the window with tears rolling down his cheeks. "What do you see, Mr. Moody?" asked one of the men.*
>
> *"I see countless thousands of souls that will one day spend eternity in hell if they do not find the Savior."*
>
> *Obviously, D. L. Moody saw people differently than the average observer does. And because he saw eternal souls where others saw only people strolling in a park, Moody approached life with a different agenda."*

3

Be Clean & Neat

Your first impression is powerful. Within seconds of meeting you, every prospect makes unconscious judgments about you. Are you a threat? Are you trustworthy? Why should I listen?

If you don't look like you have your act together, why should they trust you with something as important as their eternal destination? They probably won't.

Make a good impression with your outward appearance to increase the chance that people will listen to you. Allow me to give some obvious suggestions.

- Dress neatly in matching clothes that have been washed and ironed.
- Choose an appropriate hairstyle that honors the Lord. Keep your hair clean and neat.
- Brush your teeth.

Winning Souls Step-By-Step

- Freshen your breath with mouthwash or mints.

- Use deoderant.

- Don't use excessive cologne or perfume.

- Carry a clean handkerchief to be used when necessary. They are useful to wipe noses, clean up messes, and offer to people who are crying.

Once again, we should be soul conscious and witness to as many people as possible as we go throughout our week. However, make an extra effort to be clean and neat during your scheduled soul-winning times.

4

Carry Gospel Tracts

Do you know who passes out Gospel tracts? Christians who carry them! Gospel tracts are a powerful and reliable way to share the truth of salvation. You can use them to start a conversation about the Lord. Also, they are the perfect tool to give to someone when time doesn't allow you to witness to them thoroughly.

Every church should have high-quality Gospel tracts customized with their information. You can order the Gospel tracts we design at addtoyourfaith.com.

Winning Souls Step-By-Step

5

Carry A New Testament

God's Word changes lives. We must use it to win people to Christ.

1 Peter 1:23

Being born again, not of corruptible seed, but of incorruptible, by the word of God, which liveth and abideth for ever.

Every Christian should have a New Testament to carry with them while they go soul winning. I believe this practice is better than carrying a whole Bible. Many unchurched people will be intimidated if you approach them having a big Bible. A New Testament is the perfect size to carry with you. It allows you to share the Gospel in almost any situation.

You can win people to Christ from a Gospel tract. You can quote the Bible to any willing listener. However, it is always preferable to show a prospect the Scriptures from a Bible or New Testament.

6

Mark Your New Testament

Highlight the verses you will use to win people to Christ. Draw a map through the New Testament by writing the address of the verse you will go to next by the current verse you are looking at. Here is how to mark your Bible using the modified Romans Road approach we teach.

Next to 1 John 5:13, write Romans 3:10.

Next to Romans 3:10, write Romans 3:23.

Next to Romans 3:23, write Romans 6:23a.

Next to Romans 6:23a, write Revelation 21:8b.

Next to Revelation 21:8, write Romans 6:23b.

Next to Romans 6:23b, write Romans 5:8.

Next to Romans 5:8, write Romans 10:9-10.

Next to Romans 10:9-10 write Romans 10:13.

Winning Souls Step-By-Step

You can use the same system to mark the verses that you intend to use to provide assurance of salvation, show the importance of going to church, explain the need for a public profession, and teach believer's baptism. Those verses are found in the appropriate sections in this book.

7

Go Two-By-Two

There are several good reasons to go soul winning in groups of two.

It is Scriptural. Jesus sent out the apostles two by two.

> *Mark 6:7*
>
> *"And he called unto him the twelve, and began to send them forth by two and two; and gave them power over unclean spirits;"*

It is wise.

There is strength in unity. Soul winners can encourage one another.

It is efficient.

New soul winners need to be trained by experienced ones. This is God's plan.

It is safe.

Winning Souls Step-By-Step

In today's mixed-up world, you can be treated as guilty until proven innocent when accused of wrongdoing. Having an extra set of eyes and ears provides a critical layer of security.

8

Go With Different People

There are three essential reasons to go soul winning with different people.

Soul winning binds the hearts of those who go together. Therefore, going with different people will connect you to more people in the church.

Going with different people allows you to train new soul winners.

Going with different people enables you to learn from others. Every soul winner has different approaches, illustrations, and personalities. You will grow as a personal soul winner when you watch others do it.

Winning Souls Step-By-Step

9

Claim The Holy Spirit's Power Before You Go

The Holy Spirit is the source of our spiritual power. Soul winning is spiritual business. The Holy Spirit gives us boldness, reminds us of what to say, convicts sinners, and converts the soul. Without the power of the Holy Ghost, we will fail.

Acts 1:8

"But ye shall receive power, after that the Holy Ghost is come upon you: and ye shall be witnesses unto me both in Jerusalem, and in all Judaea, and in Samaria, and unto the uttermost part of the earth."

Yield to the Holy Ghost. Die to self. Confess any known sin. Empty your heart of all pride and self-will, asking the Holy Spirit to fill you. Claim the fullness of the Spirit by praying a prayer like the following.

"Dear Lord, I claim the fullness of the Holy Spirit before I go.

I pray that you will give me the boldness to say what I should, the love to say it like Christ, and the power so that what I say will make a difference. Go before me to soften hearts and open doors. Help me win someone to You today. Amen."

10

Go Believing

This one practice could change your life. In Matthew 8:13, Jesus told the Centurion, "As thou hast believed, so be it done unto thee."

How would your soul winning go if Christ made you the same promise? Too often, we go soul winning in doubt and unbelief. If you don't expect to see someone saved, you won't!

God said that He would save people if we would go. Do you believe His promise? Go believing. Expect people to listen. Expect God to work supernaturally. Expect to see someone saved and keep talking to them until it happens.

11

Talk To The First Person You See

Once on soul patrol, talk to the first person you see. This practice helps you shake off the cobwebs and dive right into your soul-winning time.

Soul winning is a spiritual battle. Satan is working against you. The longer you wait to talk to someone, the more difficult it becomes.

Committed soul winners love to witness for Christ - once they get started. Many effective soul winners have difficulty getting started but don't want to stop after speaking to someone about the Lord.

Don't drive across town to see a prospect who may or may not be home while driving past people outside. Talk to some folks first, then make your visits.

Decisive action is the remedy for fear and procrastination. Break the ice and talk to the first person you see.

27

12

Be Charming

How you approach a prospect will significantly affect the outcome of the conversation. Being charming disarms people and allows you to connect with them more easily. Charm is a lost art, but anyone can be charming by following a few simple guidelines.

Be courteous, kind, and gentle. Smile warmly. Exude positive energy with a good attitude. Genuinely care about the person to whom you are speaking. Make eye contact with a friendly countenance. Smile with your eyes. Be humble yet confident. Find things you have in common. Talk to them like an old friend.

If you can build these traits into your character, you will connect with people more easily.

13

Be Complimentary

People love to hear good things about themselves and their lives. Make it a habit to find something to brag about when addressing a prospect. If you are at someone's door, you can comment on how lovely their house is or how beautiful the landscaping looks. If you are walking in the park, you can comment on the dog the prospect is walking or the child in the stroller.

Allow me to give you a word of caution. There is a difference between genuine compliments and hypocritical flattery. Don't lie. Don't say nice things only because you have an agenda. Simply find something you appreciate and comment on that sincerely.

14

Be Wise About Going In A Home

We must exercise wisdom about going into homes. Never go into a home when a person of the opposite sex is home alone. Also, never go into a home when teens or children are home alone. In our crazy world, unfounded accusations can cause tremendous pain and suffering. You can always go back to the house another time.

Winning Souls Step-By-Step

15

Don't Get Distracted

Don't stop soul-winning efforts to argue with someone from a different religion or belief that has no intention of getting saved. Talk to them long enough to see if they are open to the Gospel, but don't get bogged down into an hour-long debate. Use your time to plant the seed of salvation and seek people under conviction.

Also, be careful about fellowshipping for too long with believers. If you meet a person who is born again and happily attending a Bible-preaching church, don't spend the rest of your soul-winning time talking. You can set up an appointment to do that another time. Stay after sinners.

16

Be A Good Listener

There is always a place in the world for a good listener. People need to be heard. If you listen to a person with genuine interest, they usually respond in kind. Use the F.O.R.M. framework to start a conversation and transition to the Gospel.

Family – ask about the prospect's family and children.

Occupation – ask where the prospect works and how long he has been employed there.

Recreation – ask the prospect about their interests and hobbies.

Message – transition to the Gospel presentation.

17

Choose One Person To Do The Talking

When two people go soul winning together, it is essential that one do the talking and the other be the silent partner. A silent partner helps in six important ways.

1.   A silent partner provides safety.
Satan will use any trick in his book to trip up or defame a servant of the Lord. The presence of a silent partner protects against evil and accusation.

2.   A silent partner offers assistance.
The Devil loves to interrupt soul winning. The silent partner can intercept someone who interrupts, play with children, pet the dog, etc., allowing the conversation to continue.

3.   A silent partner supplies encouragement.
A partner is encouraging when people are not responding favorably, or the results of your efforts are not visible. Fellowship and Camaraderie are sweet when serving the

Lord together.

4.   A silent partner supplies aid.

Sometimes a soul winner gets confused by a question or doesn't know how to continue the conversation. A silent partner can help.

5.   A silent partner prays.

The silent partner should pray God gives wisdom to the speaker and for the soul of the listener.

6.   A silent partner learns.

Most soul winners begin their public ministry by being a silent partner for someone more experienced. The silent partner should watch and learn. The skilled soul winner should teach what he has learned.

If two experienced soul winners go together, they can switch roles after each conversation. This tactic is an efficient way to ensure each partner takes turns as the lead and silent partner.

18

Stay On The Subject

Questions may arise when you are presenting the Gospel. A wise Christian should never be intimidated by questions. Questions help people learn. However, the Bible also warns about getting trapped debating "foolish questions, and genealogies, and contentions, and strivings about the law."

Titus 3:9

"But avoid foolish questions, and genealogies, and contentions, and strivings about the law; for they are unprofitable and vain."

A prospect may ask questions such as "Where did Cain get his wife?" or "Do you think the Antichrist is alive today?" or "Do you think it's OK to get a tattoo?"

When questions arise, simply say, "That is a good question. Allow me to finish showing you how to go to Heaven, and then I will answer any questions you have."

I have never had someone who trusted Christ and then cared about any questions they asked at the beginning of the conversation.

If they don't trust Christ, answer all their questions and objections with Scripture. Either way, stay on the subject. Preach Christ. Nothing else matters if they remain lost, and the questions will go away if they get saved. Stay on the subject.

19

Get Them Lost

Only sinners need a Saviour. Many people today don't see the need for salvation because they don't see their sinfulness in the sight of a holy God. We must get people lost before they will want to get saved. That means we must show them from the Bible that they have broken God's law and are condemned to eternal judgment unless they trust Christ.

Let's do a thought experiment.

Imagine you are on a commercial airplane, and the stewardess begins making each person put on a 90-pound parachute. The stewardess explains that there is a .0001% chance that you will be killed on this flight, so you need to wear the parachute.

How would you respond? I imagine that you would not be happy. I mean, how many times have you flown and been safe? How often do planes crash anyway? You've known

43

a lot of people that have flown many times who have never died, and they did not have to wear a parachute. You would probably think the policy was ridiculous!

Now imagine another scenario.

You're flying 600 mph at 33,000 feet. The stewardess comes to your seat and says the plane is going to crash so you must put on a parachute. Your questions would probably be very different, wouldn't they? How do I put this thing on? How does it work? Do you have one for each of my family members?

You see, the knowledge of impending doom changes your perspective entirely. It's the same with sinners. If they think they're OK without Jesus, why would they ever trust Him? However, if they know they are lost and undone, condemned to eternal fire because of their sin, you will have their full attention.

Repentance for salvation occurs when a sinner changes his mind about the Sovereign, the Saviour, and their sinfulness. When a man realizes that he is a hopeless sinner condemned to Hell as the just punishment for his offences against a holy God, he will recognize his need for the Saviour.

Find a way to get sinners lost. Use the Ten Commandments. Everyone has told a lie. That's an easy place to start. When someone tells me that they have never told a lie or sinned, I simply ask if they want me to ask their mother or spouse if that statement is true. Usually, the prospect smiles sheepishly and admits that they would rather me not ask.

20

Stay In One Or Two Books Of The Bible

When you witness to someone, you are the Bible expert in that situation. You may have confidence bouncing around the Bible to different books and passages; however, your prospect will not. Make it easy for them to follow you by staying in one or two books of the Bible. Use a marked New Testament with highlighted verses.

21

Transition The Conversation To The Gospel

Transitions are important in every endeavor. The same is true in soul winning. Smooth transitions improve the possibility of success. Botched transitions are single points of failure that multiply the likelihood of disappointment.

We have an entire chapter with proven transition statements in our more comprehensive book, "Winning Souls God's Way: A Manual For Confident Soul Winning." It will be released in 2023 and be available at addtoyourfaith.com.

The proper use of effective transition statements will dramatically increase your soul-winning proficiency. We will teach you some effective transitions in the following chapter.

Sections 21 through 32 give a step-by-step instructions of how to win a soul to Christ. The quotes represent your part of the conversation. Instructions are given in parenthesis.

Blank pages can be used for notes.

22

Ask This Powerful Transition Question

"If You Died Today, Are You 100% Sure That You Would Go To Heaven Or Do You Have Some Doubt About It?"

(If they contend they already attend a church use the following statement.)

"It's important to go to church, but it is more important to go to Heaven. If you were to die today, do you know for sure that you are going to Heaven?"

Winning Souls Step-By-Step

23

Explain He Can Know For Sure

"Did you know that there is a verse in the Bible that tells you that you can know for sure that you are going to Heaven? Can I show it to you?"

"I have shown this verse to people that have gone to church for over 50 years, and they had never seen it. Look at this amazing verse."

1 John 5:13

"These things have I written unto you that believe on the name of the Son of God; that ye may know that ye have eternal life, and that ye may believe on the name of the Son of God."

Winning Souls Step-By-Step

24

Peak Interest With Four Things He Must Know

"As you just read, the Bible says you can know for sure that you are going to Heaven. Here's another amazing fact. There are only four things you need to know to go to Heaven. You probably already have heard of three of them. That means that you are only one step away from Heaven!"

25

Explain Everyone Is A Sinner

"For example, the Bible says the first thing we need to know to go to Heaven is that no one is perfect."

Romans 3:10

"As it is written, There is none righteous, no, not one:"

"This verse means that no one is perfect. You believe that, don't you?

"The Bible tells us why no one is perfect. It's because we have all sinned."

Romans 3:23

"For all have sinned, and come short of the glory of God;"

"To sin is to break God's law. For example, God gave the Ten Commandments to mankind. If we have broken one, we are guilty of all because we are not perfect. Have you ever taken something that wasn't yours? That's stealing. Have you ever lied? We all have. Since we have sinned, we fall short of the glory of God. That means that we cannot go to Heaven because of our sins.

We can't go to Heaven on our own any more than we could jump over the Grand Canyon in our own strength."

26

Show The Price Of Sin

"The second thing the Bible says that we must know to go to Heaven is that there is a penalty for sin.

Romans 6:23

"For the wages of sin is death..."

"If we robbed a bank today and got caught, we would go to jail. If we get caught speeding in our car, we will get a ticket. Spiritually, we have sinned against God, and we always get caught.

"We work to get paid, right? What we earn is called wages. How would you feel if you worked all week and didn't get paid? God is just. He must pay us what we have earned for our sins.

"The wages for our sin is death. The Bible says there are two kinds of death. The first death is the death of the body. Each body will die because they are tainted with sin. The second death is the torment of the soul in Hell."

Revelation 21:8b

"... and all liars, shall have their part in the lake which burneth with fire and brimstone: which is the second death."

"Have you ever told a lie? I have too. We all have. That means that all of us deserve the second death, which is eternal torment in Hell. What is Hell like? Imagine an ocean of lava and fire. If we don't accept Christ as our Saviour, our souls will be cast into this lake of fire, burning forever but will never stop existing. Hell is eternal torment.

"The good news is that no one has to go to Hell. In fact, if you go to Hell, it will be over Christ's dead body!"

27

Reveal Christ Died To Pay For Our Sin

"The third thing that Bible says that we must know is that Jesus Christ died on the Cross to pay for our sins. Look at this verse again."

Romans 6:23

"For the wages of sin is death; but the gift of God is eternal life through Jesus Christ our Lord."

"God wants to give you a gift. What is that gift? Eternal life! Eternal life means living forever in eternal bliss in Heaven with God.

"How do we get that gift? Through Jesus!"

Romans 5:8

"But God commendeth his love toward us, in that, while we were yet sinners, Christ died for us."

"The word "commendeth" means demonstrated or proved.

God proved His love toward us by dying on the Cross to pay for our sins. There is no greater love than to die for someone so that they can be saved.

"Look back at Romans 6:23. We have earned the penalty of eternal death because of our sins. Christ paid the price for our sins on the Cross.

"Let's imagine that you owed the IRS $100,000 in back taxes. While we are talking, the police and IRS agents break down the door and start dragging you to prison until you pay the debt. But you can't pay the debt because you are in prison. You will be in prison forever! But what if I stopped the IRS agents by saying I would pay the bill? I take out my checkbook and write a check to the IRS in your name for $100,000. Let me ask you a question. Does the IRS care who writes the check? No! They will be satisfied if the debt is paid in full. I can pay your debt, and you can go free.

"This illustration explains what Jesus did for you on the Cross. You owed a debt of sin that you could never pay, so Jesus Christ paid for your sin on the Cross. If you ask Him to save you, He will settle your debt and reserve your home in Heaven. Isn't that amazing?!

"Look back on Romans 6:23 one more time. Notice that eternal life is a gift. What if I offered to give you this Bible if you gave me $25? Would it be a gift? No, you would be paying for it. If I said, "I will give you this Bible if you wash my car," would it be a gift? No, you would be working for it. You cannot buy a gift or work for it. A gift is something someone else pays for and offers you with no strings attached.

"Eternal life is a gift. You cannot work to earn it, nor can you pay for it. Christ paid for it and offers it to you free today.

"When someone offers you a gift, you have a choice. You can choose to accept it or reject it.

"What if I offered you a 2022 Corvette Stingray convertible (retails for $91,000) with free gas and insurance for life? This car goes 0-60 in 2.9 seconds, has a top speed of 194 miles per hour, and looks amazing.

(Offer what vehicle would delight the person with whom you are talking. It could be a truck or a Mercedes.)

What if it was completely paid for, and all you had to do was accept it? You would take it in a heartbeat, right? You would be a fool not to accept it! Sadly, God offers something of so much more value, eternal life, and many people will reject it. How foolish!"

28

Accept Christ As Personal Saviour Through Faith

"Let me show you one more passage of Scripture before I go. There is only one more thing you must know to know for sure you are going to Heaven."

Romans 10:9–10

"That if thou shalt confess with thy mouth the Lord Jesus, and shalt believe in thine heart that God hath raised him from the dead, thou shalt be saved. For with the heart man believeth unto righteousness; and with the mouth confession is made unto salvation."

"These verses tell us what saving faith looks like.

Saving faith says, "I believe that Jesus is Who He said He is. He is the Son of God Who died on the Cross to pay for my sin, was buried, and rose again. He is the Lord Jesus.

"Saving faith is believing in your heart. My preacher used to say that many people will miss Heaven by about 18 inches.

That's about the distance between the head and the heart. It is not enough to believe the facts about Jesus Christ in your head. The devils believe that, but they are not going to Heaven.

We must believe in Jesus Christ in our hearts. What does that mean?"

29

Get In The Wheelbarrow

"Listen to this powerful illustration to explain what it means to 'believe in your heart.'

"In 1859, daredevil Charles Blondin became the first man to walk across Niagara Falls on a tightrope. The three-inch cable stretched 1,100 feet wide, 160 feet above the gorge, and had a steep climb at both ends sagging in the middle. He had no safety equipment.

"Imagine walking the wet tightrope with heavy winds beating your body, thick mist affecting your vision, and thundering sounds all around you.

"On the day of the stunt, thousands of people gathered to watch the daredevil perform the risky act. He was so sure of his success that he offered to carry a volunteer on his back.

"He completed the dangerous task to the cheers of the enthralled crowd. It took about 17 minutes.

"He went on to cross the gorge near the falls a few more times. Each time he would invent a new way to cross it. He walked across it blindfolded, carrying his manager on his back, and pushing a wheelbarrow on the cable.

"Suppose that we were in the crowd watching the event. Blondin had successfully crossed the falls. We believed he could do it. We just saw him. That is head belief.

"Now, suppose that Blondin put the wheelbarrow in front of him on the cable and offered to take you across. Would you get in? Only if you truly believed in your heart!

"Trusting Jesus Christ 'in your heart' means that you not only believe the facts that He died on the Cross to pay for your sin, was buried, and rose again. It is trusting Him to save you! It is trusting the eternal destiny of your soul to Christ alone. It is getting in the spiritual wheelbarrow trusting Him to save YOUR soul.

"Will you get in Jesus' wheelbarrow?"

(You don't need to relate every detail of the story for it to be effective. Tell the story in your own words and make it real to the prospect.)

30

Reveal He Is Only One Step From Heaven

"(NAME) you are only one step away from going to Heaven. Allow me to show you one final verse. Look at Romans 10:13."

Romans 10:13

"For whosoever shall call upon the name of the Lord shall be saved."

"This verse explains that God will save anyone who believes the Gospel enough to confess with their mouth that Jesus Christ is the Saviour and call upon Him asking for forgiveness of sins. When you call upon the Lord in faith, you will be saved from the second death and rescued from Hell. That's good news, isn't it?"

31

Make It Personal

"Let's read Romans 10:13 again."

Romans 10:13

"For whosoever shall call upon the name of the Lord shall be saved."

"This verse explains that anyone who believes the Gospel enough to call on Jesus Christ for salvation will be saved. You will be saved from the second death and saved from Hell. Jesus Christ will save anyone who accepts Him as their Saviour trusting Him to get them to Heaven."

"Let's read Romans 10:13 one more time, putting your name in place of "whosoever."

"For if (NAME) shall call upon the name of the Lord (NAME) shall be saved."

"Every person has two choices. Either you will have to pay

69

for your sins and be condemned to Hell forever to pay for your sin debt, or you will trust Jesus Christ to save you from Hell and give you a home in Heaven. No one in their right mind wants to go to Hell, do they?"

32

Review The 4 Points To Make Sure The Prospect Understands

"Let's review the four things you must believe to know for sure you are going to Heaven."

1. "No one is perfect, are they? You are a sinner too, right?"

2. "The Bible says that the wages of sin is death. We all deserve to go to Hell, don't we? According to the Bible, where would you go if you died without Christ?"

3. "The Bible says that Jesus Christ died on the Cross so we can go to Heaven, doesn't it? They buried Him, and three days later, what happened? That's right. He arose from the dead."

4. "The Bible says that we must believe the Gospel in our hearts to go to Heaven, doesn't it? If you were to do your part and call on the Lord in faith, He would do His part and save you from Hell, wouldn't He?"

Winning Souls Step-By-Step

(Notice how we ask close-ended questions with an obvious answer. We want to make sure prospects understand and believe, not stump them. If they don't believe the doctrine, they will tell you. If the person is unsure of a doctrine, provide more Bible verses until they understand or the conversation ends.)

33

Invite The Prospect To Trust Christ Right Now

"Since you believe those four things, you already know everything you need to in order to go to Heaven, but there is one thing you must do. You must put your faith in the death, burial, and resurrection of Jesus Christ for salvation once and for all. You can exercise saving faith by asking Jesus to save you and forgive you, right now.

(Transition to the sinner's prayer with this question.)

"(NAME), If Jesus would take you just as you are, forgive all your sins, and give you a home in Heaven when you die, wouldn't you like to ask Him to save you?"

(Explain That You Will Pray, Then Help Him Pray.)

"When I wanted to get saved, I didn't know how to pray, so someone helped me. I can help you word a prayer. It's not the words that save you. The words just point to the faith in your heart.

Let me say a prayer for you. Then I will help you word a prayer of salvation to Jesus. Let's pray in faith and ask Christ to be your Saviour. Wouldn't that be a wonderful thing?"

(Ask them to bow their heads and close their eyes. Pray a simple prayer thanking God for allowing you to meet the prospect. While praying compliment the prospect's desire to be saved and ask God to save them. Stop praying, don't say amen, and keep your head bowed. Then say:)

"Now, with our heads bowed and eyes closed, God is looking on from Heaven. He sees us and knows our hearts. Since you want to receive Jesus as your Saviour, I will help you word a prayer, and He will hear you. If you'd like to be saved, pray this prayer with me out loud to Jesus, mean the words with all your heart." (Say the following prayer phrase by phrase, waiting for the sinner to repeat after you.)

"Dear Jesus, I know I'm a sinner, and I can't go to Heaven on my own. But I believe You died on the Cross to pay for my sin and rose again from the dead. I confess that I am a sinner. I don't want to go to Hell. Please forgive all my sins and take me to Heaven when I die. Right now, I am trusting You as my only hope for Heaven. Thank You, Jesus, for saving me. Amen."

(CONGRATULATIONS! You have just won a soul to Christ! Great job! The following sections will teach you how to work with your new convert, helping them to grow in grace as they follow Jesus.)

34

Give The New Convert Biblical Assurance Of Salvation

You must leave a new convert with the assurance that God will keep His Word and that their eternal destiny is settled through saving faith in Jesus Christ. If not, Satan will paralyze them with fear and false doctrine.

We started our soul-winning plan with the idea that we could know for sure we were going to Heaven. Use any combination of the verses below to settle the matter in the new believer's heart.

After they pray to trust Christ, say, "You meant that in your heart, didn't you? Let me share with you something exciting."

Since we finished our Gospel presentation with Romans 10:13, it is an excellent place to begin giving a new believer the assurance of salvation. Let's pick up the conversation where we left off.

"Let's look at Romans 10:13 again."

Romans 10:13

"For whosoever shall call upon the name of the Lord shall be saved."

(Reread the verse inserting their name.)

"For if [First Name] shall call upon the name of the Lord [First Name] shall be saved.

"Does this verse say you might be saved, or will hopefully be saved? No, it says you SHALL be saved.

"According to this verse, you are....saved?"

(Point to the word saved and wait for them to say it.)

"Where do saved people go when they die?" Let them answer, "Heaven!"

"If you had died before you were saved, where would you have spent eternity?" It is sobering to watch them say, Hell.

"According to this verse, where will you go NOW?"

(It is wonderful to watch their face light up as they say, "Heaven!")

Let's look at Titus 1:2.

Titus 1:2

"In hope of eternal life, which God, that cannot lie, promised before the world began;"

"This verse says that God can't lie, doesn't it? God promised to take you to Heaven if you believed in Him. He will keep His promise, won't He?

"Here's another excellent verse about the salvation you just

76

received by trusting Jesus."

John 1:12

"But as many as received him, to them gave he power to become the sons of God, even to them that believe on his name:"

"This verse explains that you became God's child when you accepted Christ. When a child disobeys a parent, does the parent build a big fire in the backyard and throw the kid in it? Of course, not! A good parent will chasten and correct a child, but they would die to protect them. God is a better Father than any human father. When we disobey our Heavenly Father, He lovingly corrects us. He does not send us to Hell."

"Let's look at John 3:36."

John 3:36

"He that believeth on the Son hath everlasting life: and he that believeth not the Son shall not see life; but the wrath of God abideth on him."

"God promises eternal life to those who believe in Christ for salvation. Did you accept Jesus as your Saviour? How long is everlasting life? Can you lose something that lasts forever?"

Give as many verses as the Holy Spirit leads. Sometimes a few verses are sufficient. Other times, they need more assurance to dispel false doctrines they have heard over the years.

Below are more verses of assurance you can use if necessary.

77

Winning Souls Step-By-Step

1 John 5:13 "...that ye may know that ye have eternal life..." Reread the verse inserting their name like you did in Romans 10:13.

Hebrews 13:5 "...I will never leave thee or forsake thee."

John 5:24 "...shall not come into condemnation."

35

Create A Record
Of The Decision

Write their name with the date of their salvation on a Spiritual Birth Certificate or a Gospel tract from your church. Explain that the tract includes some of the same verses you showed them. They can review the verses and remember the time and date if they ever doubt their salvation.

Take out a Convert Card (available at addtoyourfaith.com) and tell them you will be praying for them. As you write their name (they already gave it to you when you wrote it on the tract), ask them if there is anything specific you can pray about for them.

Get their address and phone number to write on the card so you can follow up.

36

Ask The Convert To Promise God That He Will Come To Church

Every Christian should attend a local church. The Bible is clear that if we are not faithful to a local church after salvation, we will not be able to maintain the Christian life without wavering.

New converts are born again as new creatures in Christ. However, this new creature is still wrapped in a robe of flesh with sinful habits and desires. We must work with new converts to provide encouragement and support to overcome the old man and live in the power of the new man.

Follow these instructions to get your converts to church after you win them to Christ.

1. Use the same love, diligence, and concern to get him to church as you used to get him saved.

   Galatians 4:19

   "My little children, of whom I travail in birth again

until Christ be formed in you,"

1 Thessalonians 2:6–8

"Nor of men sought we glory, neither of you, nor yet of others, when we might have been burdensome, as the apostles of Christ. But we were gentle among you, even as a nurse cherisheth her children: So being affectionately desirous of you, we were willing to have imparted unto you, not the Gospel of God only, but also our own souls, because ye were dear unto us."

2. Teach him that God wants saved people to go to church.

   Hebrews 10:23–25

   "Let us hold fast the profession of our faith without wavering; (for he is faithful that promised;) And let us consider one another to provoke unto love and to good works: Not forsaking the assembling of ourselves together, as the manner of some is; but exhorting one another: and so much the more, as ye see the day approaching."

3. Emphasize that he should go to the church where he learned how to go to Heaven.

4. Explain your church services and how they are conducted. Usually, new converts have no idea how an exciting Baptist church is different than the cold dead churches they have visited in the past. Tell the convert how your church is different and what to expect.

   • Our church is friendly.

- Our pastor makes the Bible come alive.

- We sing hymns that draw us close to God.

- Our church is like a family. We laugh together, cry together, and learn together.

- Pastor gives an invitation at the end of the service to apply what we've learned about to our lives. Some people will walk the aisle to pray or make decisions, while others pray in their seats.

5. Show them that they should not be ashamed of Jesus. Once they get saved, they can show they are not ashamed of Christ or His words by attending a Bible-believing church.

   Luke 9:26

   "For whosoever shall be ashamed of me and of my words, of him shall the Son of man be ashamed, when he shall come in his own glory, and in his Father's, and of the holy angels."

6. Stress the importance of going to church for Jesus. "After all that Jesus Christ went through to save our souls, is it too much for us to attend a church service for Him?"

7. Ask them to visit at least one time.

8. Let them know there is no obligation to join the church.

9. Tell him that your church has guests regularly. He will fit right in.

10. Let him know that you will host him the entire time and show him around. He can sit with you in the

service.

11. Explain that you will give him a Bible when he comes to church.

12. If he is reluctant, ask him to visit one time.

13. Invite him to breakfast before church or lunch after church.

14. Ask him to be your personal guest. Be very kind and persuasive.

15. Once he agrees to attend your church, ask him to promise God he will come. Then pray for him.

    "I'm glad you told me you will come to church this Sunday. Will you promise God, right now, that you will come? Great! Let's pray one more time. 'Lord, thank you for John getting saved today. I'm glad he is going to Heaven because he trusted in You as his Saviour. He just promised You that he is coming to church this Sunday. I pray that You would protect him and remind him of his promise throughout the week. Amen.'"

16. Make an appointment to pick him up next Sunday.

17. Before you leave, get his phone number. Text him on Saturday. Call him on Sunday morning about an hour and a half before it is time to pick him up. If he says he has changed his mind, remind him of his promise to God, and persuade him again to come.

18. Be a friend to the new convert. Have him to your home for refreshments or for dinner. Take him out to lunch or invite him for coffee.

Overcoming Objections

One of the jobs of the soul winner is to help remove the excuses that would keep the convert from attending church.

1. If he says he cannot come on Sunday morning, invite him to come on Sunday evening. Remember to have him promise God that he will come.

2. If he can't come this week, tell him you will check with him next week.

3. If he is reluctant to come to church, ask him if he genuinely trusted Jesus Christ. If so, he should be glad to assemble with God's people.

4. If he says he will go to his family member's church, kindly remind him who led him to the Lord. "If God sent someone from our church to show you how to go to Heaven, doesn't it make sense that God would want you to come to our church?"

37

Pick Him Up or Meet Him In The Parking Lot

Be responsible for getting your new convert to church on the first Sunday. If he says he would like to drive, mention that you want to bring him the first time. Explain that you enjoy bringing guests to church and that he will be doing you a favor to let you pick him up.

If you cannot pick him up, arrange for someone else to do so. In that event, tell him where you will meet him in church to sit with him.

If he insists on driving, set a time to meet him in the church parking lot and walk him into the building as your personal guest.

Text or call him during the week to stay in touch.

Don't be surprised when a new convert backs out of his commitment to come to church on the first Sunday. Sadly, only about 25% of those who promise to come to church will make it that first week. Due to a lack of character in this generation and the attempts of Satan to hinder the new believer's growth, you will have to deal with obstacles.

Call the convert on Saturday night to confirm.

If you are picking them up, you could say: *"I'm so happy that you are coming to church as my guest tomorrow. Did I tell you I would pick you up at 8:40 am or 8:45 am?"*

If they are meeting you at church you could say: *"I'm so happy that you are coming to church as my guest tomorrow. Did I ask you to meet me in the parking lot or at the door?"*

On Sunday morning, you can call or text them to say: *"I just want to make sure the Devil didn't sneak in and shut off your alarm clock. It's a beautiful day to worship the Lord!"*

38

Treat The New Convert As A VIP On His First Visit

People are reluctant to go to new places and meet new people. Make the experience as pleasant as possible by hosting their entire experience.

1. Meet him in the parking lot if he didn't ride to church with you.

2. Show him around the building and sit with him in church.

3. Introduce him to people you pass in the building.

4. Sit with him in the service.

5. Share your hymnal during the song service.

6. Share your Bible during the sermon.

7. Show approval during the sermon by nodding your head and saying, "Amen."

8. Ask if they have anything you can pray about during

the invitation.

9. Help them make a profession of faith during the invitation.

10. Walk them to their vehicle after the service.

11. Tell them you will be in touch this week.

12. Be a true friend to the convert.

39

Lead Him To Make A Public Profession Of Faith During The Invitation

Satan will not be happy that you have won a sinner to Christ. He will do everything he can to paralyze the new convert from growing in grace or making an eternal difference.

Shame is a reliable tool in Satan's evil arsenal. He works to make the convert ashamed of the Saviour and keep the miracle of salvation to himself. We must not let that happen. We must help the new believer be open and excited about his faith immediately. Encourage him to tell someone about his newfound faith on the day of his salvation. Insist that he tell his friends and family about his faith that day.

A public profession of faith is a powerful way to encourage a new believer to share his faith. Also, it excites the church family to see new believers walk the aisle, encourages the members to get busy sharing their faith, and reminds apathetic Christians that people are still getting saved.

Winning Souls Step-By-Step

Use these tips to help your convert make a public profession of faith during the invitation at your church.

1. Talk to your new convert when they are at church.

2. Explain Matthew 10:32-33.

   "Whosoever therefore shall confess me before men, him will I confess also before my Father which is in heaven. But whosoever shall deny me before men, him will I also deny before my Father which is in heaven."

3. Explain that we must let people know that we are saved. We could run up and down the street shouting at strangers, but that would be weird. The easiest way to show that we are not ashamed of Christ is to let people know at church.

4. Explain that the church members will completely understand their decision and rejoice with them.

5. Ask if you can let the pastor know of his great decision to trust Christ.

6. Explain that you will walk down the aisle with them during the invitation and let the pastor know.

7. Assure the convert that he will not have to give a speech or say anything in front of the congregation.

8. Walk down the aisle with him during the invitation.

9. Introduce him to the pastor.

10. Tell the pastor of his decision.

11. The pastor will confirm the decision with the convert and encourage him in the Lord.

12. The pastor will ask, "Do you mind if I let people know that you accepted Christ so they can rejoice with you?"

13. The pastor will have you or the name-taker fill out a decision card as he conducts the rest of the invitation.

14. This is an excellent time to explain the need for believer's baptism.

15. The decision slip will be handed to the pastor.

16. At the close of the invitation, the pastor will explain to the congregation that the convert accepted Christ. He will ask the members to rejoice with the new believer with a hearty amen. Unless the convert is getting baptized, the pastor will ask the soul winner and convert to remain at the front for a few minutes after the service so people can stop by to congratulate him.

Overcoming Objections

Once again, one of the duties of the soul winner is to help remove the excuses that would keep the convert from growing. Help overcome any objections to a public profession with these truths.

1. If he is shy, remind him that you will do all the talking.

2. Remind the convert that you will be with him the whole time.

3. Assure the convert that he will not have to give a speech or say anything in front of the congregation.

4. Mention that God will be pleased with this simple act.

5. Remind him of all that Christ did to purchase his salvation. Is it too much for Christ to ask the new

believer to tell others of Christ's love?

6. If the convert is unwilling to make a public profession, set up a time to meet with him during the week for discipleship. Try again next week.

If the convert is happy to be saved and willing to go to church, he will most likely be willing to profess his faith publicly with your help. Lead the new believer confidently and enjoy watching him grow in grace.

40

Encourage The New Convert To Embrace Believer's Baptism

Baptism is the next step of obedience after salvation. If a believer is not baptized, he will not grow in the grace and knowledge of the Lord.

Some soul winners tell the new convert about the need to be baptized right after the person is saved. Other soul winners wait until the convert comes to church for the first time to explain the responsibility of being baptized.

Typically, I wait until the convert comes to church, but every situation is different. Seek the Lord for wisdom as you work with each convert.

1. Convey Christ's command to be baptized.

    Matthew 28:19–20

    "Go ye therefore, and teach all nations, baptizing them in the name of the Father, and of the Son, and of the Holy Ghost: Teaching them to observe

95

all things whatsoever I have commanded you: and, lo, I am with you alway, even unto the end of the world. Amen."

2. Clarify that Biblical baptism occurs by immersion after salvation.

   Acts 8:35–39

   "Then Philip opened his mouth, and began at the same Scripture, and preached unto him Jesus. And as they went on their way, they came unto a certain water: and the eunuch said, See, here is water; what doth hinder me to be baptized? And Philip said, If thou believest with all thine heart, thou mayest. And he answered and said, I believe that Jesus Christ is the Son of God. And he commanded the chariot to stand still: and they went down both into the water, both Philip and the eunuch; and he baptized him. And when they were come up out of the water, the Spirit of the Lord caught away Philip, that the eunuch saw him no more: and he went on his way rejoicing."

3. Explain that those who were glad to be saved were baptized immediately in the Bible.

   Acts 2:41

   "Then they that gladly received his word were baptized: and the same day there were added unto them about three thousand souls."

4. Explain the symbolism of baptism.

   Water baptism does not wash away sins. It is not part of salvation. Instead, baptism is a symbol like a wedding ring. If I take my wedding ring off, I am still married. However, I wear my wedding ring to let others know that I am married. Likewise, baptism does not save us but shows others that we are saved. It is an outward symbol of an inward decision.

5. Stress the importance of attending church for Jesus.

   "If Jesus was willing to die on the Cross to pay for our sins so we can go to Heaven, we should be willing to obey Him after salvation."

6. Explain that the church has everything ready, and the pastor will guide him through the process.

7. Teach them that God is pleased when we follow Christ in baptism.

   Matthew 3:16–17

   "And Jesus, when he was baptized, went up straightway out of the water: and, lo, the heavens were opened unto him, and he saw the Spirit of God descending like a dove, and lighting upon him: And lo a voice from heaven, saying, This is my beloved Son, in whom I am well pleased."

   When Christ was baptized, God spoke from Heaven saying that He was well pleased. When we are baptized, God gives us joy and peace to convey His pleasure.

8. Encourage them to invite their friends and family to witness the baptism. This practice allows the preacher to preach a Gospel message to their lost loved ones.

9. Use a helpful brochure to teach these concepts. We recommend our brochure "Believer's Baptism: Why Every Believer Should Take The Plunge" found at addtoyourfaith.com.

41

Meet Him for Coffee Within A Week.

Ministry is relational.

You can't influence people for Christ over time if you don't have a relationship with them.

Build a relationship with the new convert. Be a genuine friend and mentor so he can grow in grace.

In today's culture, many people are more comfortable eating out than having you come in their house. If you are blessed financially, set aside money each month to take converts or young Christians out for coffee or to a restaraunt. A wise pastor may choose to put a "Discipleship Meals" line item in the budget that includes money for faithful Christians with financial trouble to invest in new converts. Most people have time or money. Few people have both. This practice allows trustworthy Christians with time to get involved in building relationships with new converts.

42

Start The New Believer On The Road To Discipleship

Salvation is the beginning of a new life. The soul winner should care for the recent convert like a parent cares for a child. We must begin them on the road to becoming a disciple immediately. Like a blacksmith, we must strike while the iron is hot. Satan will attempt to thwart their growth and derail them from God's plan.

Matthew 28:19–20

"Go ye therefore, and teach all nations, baptizing them in the name of the Father, and of the Son, and of the Holy Ghost: Teaching them to observe all things whatsoever I have commanded you: and, lo, I am with you alway, even unto the end of the world. Amen."

The Great Commission consists of three essential parts:

1. "Teach all nations" speaks of preaching the Gospel and winning souls to Christ.

2. "Baptizing them" refers to their first step of obedience after salvation to publicly identify with the Saviour.

3. "Teaching them to observe all things whatsoever I have commanded you" talks about discipling them to live like Jesus and obey His Word.

Some soul winners stop at numbers one or two. A serious soul winner continues the process seeking to disciple the new believer. Follow the steps below to get them on the road to discipleship.

1. Discipleship begins at church.

2. Baptism is the first step of obedience.

3. Sunday School is the "small groups" element of an evangelistic church.

4. Meet with them weekly, taking them through a simple personal discipleship program.

5. Start them soul winning by asking if he has any friends or family that he would like to see saved.

6. Speak to him weekly to encourage him in the faith and help with any problems he encounters.

7. The end of discipleship is when the convert is doing everything that Christ taught us to do. The goal is for your convert to become a faithful soul winner.

8. Don't give up when they don't listen.

9. Be strong when they are weak.

10. Encourage them when they stumble.

11. Be their friend.

There is great joy when you sit in church with people who

you have won to Christ and helped learn the Word. Beg God to help you win people to Christ, see your converts baptized, and watch them grow in grace.

1 Thessalonians 2:19–20

"For what is our hope, or joy, or crown of rejoicing? Are not even ye in the presence of our Lord Jesus Christ at his coming? For ye are our glory and joy."

43

Take Him Soul Winning

When the Great Commission is followed to completion, the new believer becomes a consistent personal soul winner. That is the goal!

Your new convert should be concerned about the people they know who need to be saved. Family members, coworkers, and neighbors are an excellent place to start. Ask him who he would like to be saved. Make a list. Begin praying for them with him for their souls.

Schedule a time to take him soul winning, seeking to reach those he cares about. With this obvious but often overlooked action, the new convert is placed on the road to becoming a soul winner.

Also, ask him to go with you during your church's scheduled soul winning time. With love, time, attention, and prayer, your convert can become a soul winner too.

44

How To Handle Rejection

Isaiah 53:3

"He is despised and rejected of men; A man of sorrows, and acquainted with grief: And we hid as it were our faces from him; He was despised, and we esteemed him not."

Rejection and soul winning go hand in hand. Soul winning is a spiritual intervention. Some sinners will get angry when we interrupt their lives to point out their sinful condition and need of a Saviour. Avoiding a rebuff is not a matter of being kind or using the perfect words. Rejection by sinners is an expected element of serving God.

Servants of God must learn how to deal with rejection, so they don't get discouraged or quit.

If this sinful world despised and rejected our Saviour, surely, they will mistreat His servants as well. Our Lord taught this truth to His disciples.

Mark 8:31

"And he began to teach them, that the Son of man must suffer many things, and be rejected of the elders, and of the chief priests, and scribes, and be killed, and after three days rise again."

John 15:20

"Remember the word that I said unto you, The servant is not greater than his lord. If they have persecuted me, they will also persecute you; if they have kept my saying, they will keep yours also."

Our Lord was willing to be misunderstood, despised, and rejected for our sake. We must be willing to do the same for Him.

Of course, being rejected, rebuked, or scolded by a sinner for trying to save his condemned soul from Hell is no fun. Yet, dealing with rejection is a necessary component of serving the Saviour. Allow me to give you three truths that will help you handle rejection in soul winning.

1. Doubters are rejecting Christ, not you.

Why is someone who doesn't even know you being so mean? Why is that person so angry? How could your friend or loved one with whom you have gotten along with for years be so upset? They are convicted because you brought up Christ and His Word!

The attack seems personal since they are looking at you and speaking to you. However, the attack is not about you at all. You are simply the ambassador of the One you represent. Remember, these lost souls are rejecting Him and not you.

Follow Christ's admonition to kick the dust off your feet and keep going.

Mark 6:11

"And whosoever shall not receive you, nor hear you, when ye depart thence, shake off the dust under your feet for a testimony against them. Verily I say unto you, It shall be more tolerable for Sodom and Gomorrha in the day of judgment, than for that city."

2. Your hands are clean because you obeyed the Lord.

In Old Testament cities, a watchman was deployed on the wall. His job was to warn the inhabitants of danger as they went about their day. If the watchman warned the citizens, but they didn't listen, his hands were clean. He had fulfilled his duty. Their deaths were not his fault.

On the other hand, if the watchman saw the danger coming but failed to warn the city, every death was his fault. He had blood on his hands. He was just as responsible as if he had inserted the sword into their hearts with his own hands.

The Bible likens God's people to watchmen on the wall.

Ezekiel 33:1–9

"Again the word of the LORD came unto me, saying, Son of man, speak to the children of thy people, and say unto them, When I bring the sword upon a land, if the people of the land take a man of their coasts, and set him for their watchman: If when he seeth the sword come upon the land, he blow the trumpet, and warn the people; Then whosoever heareth the sound of the trumpet, and taketh not warning; if the sword come, and take him away, his blood shall be upon his

own head. He heard the sound of the trumpet, and took not warning; his blood shall be upon him. But he that taketh warning shall deliver his soul. But if the watchman see the sword come, and blow not the trumpet, and the people be not warned; if the sword come, and take any person from among them, he is taken away in his iniquity; but his blood will I require at the watchman's hand. So thou, O son of man, I have set thee a watchman unto the house of Israel; therefore thou shalt hear the word at my mouth, and warn them from me. When I say unto the wicked, O wicked man, thou shalt surely die; if thou dost not speak to warn the wicked from his way, that wicked man shall die in his iniquity; but his blood will I require at thine hand. Nevertheless, if thou warn the wicked of his way to turn from it; if he do not turn from his way, he shall die in his iniquity; but thou hast delivered thy soul."

When sinners reject your efforts, take heart knowing that your hands are clean. You have done your job. You will never regret your obedience to the Great Commission in eternity.

3. Each rejection brings you closer to someone who is ready to receive the Gospel.

Satan uses rejection to discourage believers from spreading the life-saving message of the Gospel. Don't fall for this devilish tactic.

Mark 8:37

"Or what shall a man give in exchange for his soul?"

Christ paid the ultimate price to save souls from death and Hell. What would you give to save a soul? What is a soul worth? A soul is priceless! How many rejections would you be willing to endure for each soul that God uses you to bring to saving faith in Christ? Every sinner that gets saved is worth at least 1,000 rejections, is it not? It would be worth it if you had to endure 10,000 rejections to save a single soul! Thankfully, we don't get rejected anywhere near that many times before we win a soul. Why then do we give up so quickly?

Occasional rejection is a small price to pay to rescue the eternal souls of mankind.

When scoffers reject your soul-winning attempts, take heart! You are one person closer to finding a sinner who is under conviction.

When a prospect rejects the Saviour, shake the proverbial dust off your feet and move to the next soul. The multitudes rejected your Saviour. It is a privilege to be rejected and misunderstood for His sake. Never give up. Don't be discouraged.

You can change your mindset regarding rejection. Embrace rejection as proof that you are following in the footsteps of the Saviour. Feed on rejections as a motivation to spread the Word, realizing that you are one step closer to winning a soul.

Keep up the good work. You have a bountiful harvest of souls in your future as you faithfully share the Gospel!

Conclusion

There are many ways to win a soul. The plan presented here does not claim to be the best way or the only way. Its only claim is that it has been proven effective thousands of times.

Whether you use the plan as presented or use parts of it to enhance your own presentation, we pray that God will use this information to glorify Himself, spread the news of the glorious Gospel, and make you a more confident soul winner.

Now the work begins. You know what you need to know. You are ready. Put this book down. Go find a sinner and tell them about the Saviour!

We want to hear from you! Contact us with your testimonies of souls saved. Send your emails to info@soulwinningschool. com.

Sign up for soul-winning tips at soulwinningschool.com.

About The Author

Paul E. Chapman loves helping committed Christians reach their potential, increase their influence, and impact their world.

He has served as the pastor of Curtis Corner Baptist Church since May of 2004. He and his wife, Sarah, are blessed with three precious children. They live in a coastal community in the beautiful state of Rhode Island.

They have a passion to reach the lost Christ, to teach believers to live by faith, and to train God's people for the work of the ministry.

Sarah has had a unique blend of aggressive autoimmune diseases since 2008 that leave her bedbound 95% of the time in constant debilitating pain. Their family's testimony of faithfulness to God has been an encouragement to many.

Paul writes weekly on his website and uses his unique blend of talents for God through various ministries and enterprises.

Learn more at www.PaulEChapman.com.

thepaulechapman

More Resources Available
From Paul E Chapman

Mini-books
Ye Must Be Born Again
Abortion Atrocity

Books
Just Say No: 40 Days To Victory Over Sin
God & America
The Beauty Of Salvation: Marvel At God's
Unspeakable Gift
Praying Sinners To Jesus: How To Pray Effectively
For The Lost

Made in the USA
Middletown, DE
30 September 2023

39474125R00068